# HAUNTED PLACES
# HAUNTED ASYLUMS

WARD C
ROOM
5

WARD C
ROOM
6

ROOM
1

ROOM
2

KENNY ABDO

Fly!
An Imprint of Abdo Zoom
abdobooks.com

## abdobooks.com

Published by Abdo Zoom, a division of ABDO, P.O. Box 398166, Minneapolis, Minnesota 55439. Copyright © 2021 by Abdo Consulting Group, Inc. International copyrights reserved in all countries. No part of this book may be reproduced in any form without written permission from the publisher. Fly!™ is a trademark and logo of Abdo Zoom.

Printed in the United States of America, North Mankato, Minnesota.
052020
092020

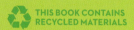

Photo Credits: AP Images, Everette Collection, iStock, Newscom, Shutterstock, ©Richie Diesterheft p15 / CC BY 2.0, ©Evan Thomas p16 / CC BY-SA 4.0
Production Contributors: Kenny Abdo, Jennie Forsberg, Grace Hansen
Design Contributors: Dorothy Toth, Neil Klinepier

**Library of Congress Control Number: 2019956178**

**Publisher's Cataloging-in-Publication Data**

Names: Abdo, Kenny, author.
Title: Haunted asylums / by Kenny Abdo
Description: Minneapolis, Minnesota : Abdo Zoom, 2021 | Series: Haunted places | Includes online resources and index.
Identifiers: ISBN 9781098221294 (lib. bdg.) | ISBN 9781644944103 (pbk.) | ISBN 9781098222277 (ebook) | ISBN 9781098222765 (Read-to-Me ebook)
Subjects: LCSH: Haunted places--Juvenile literature. | Asylums--Juvenile literature. | Ghosts--Juvenile literature. | Haunted hospitals--Juvenile literature.
Classification: DDC 133.122--dc23

# TABLE OF CONTENTS

Asylums ........................ 4

The History ..................... 8

The Haunted ................... 12

The Media ..................... 20

Glossary ...................... 22

Online Resources .............. 23

Index .......................... 24

# ASYLUMS

Tucked away from **civilization**, abandoned asylums are some of the scariest locations in the world.

These asylums were once used to house those thought to be insane. Now those same patients haunt any who dare to explore the remains.

# THE HISTORY

Hospitals with **wards** for the mentally ill date back to **Medieval** times. The first known was in Persia during the early 9th century.

Asylums dedicated to mental **disorders** were built in the 1800s. Later, they housed those who were deemed clinically insane.

Today, patients with mental illnesses are taken to hospitals where they can get better care. Mental asylums still standing have chilling pasts that linger through them like a dark shadow.

# THE HAUNTED

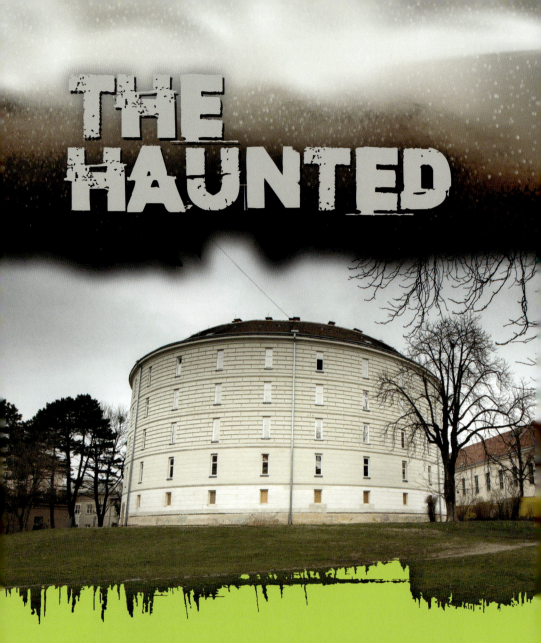

Narrenturm opened in 1784. It was Europe's first insane asylum. It was renovated into a museum in the 1970s. Tourists can witness the nastiness that took place within the walls firsthand.

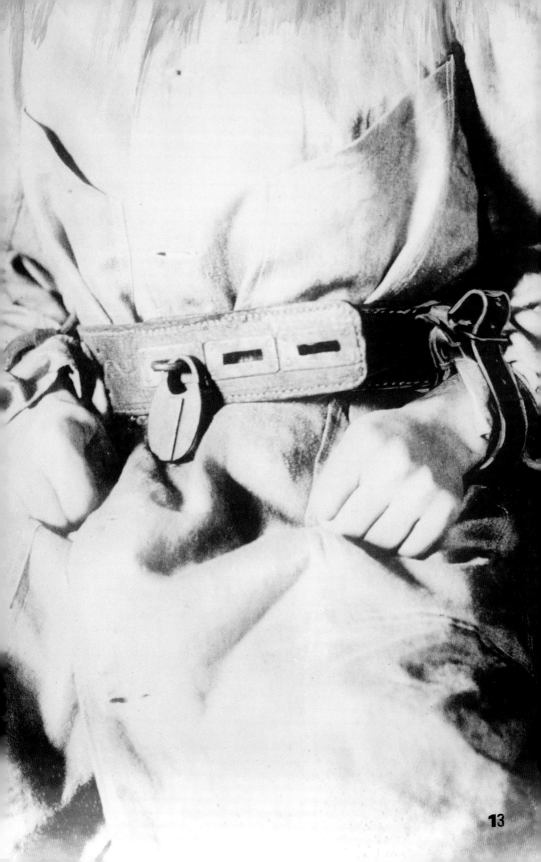

Around 1,700 patients died at Rolling Hills in New York. Tourists report unexplained screaming and doors slamming. Some also see the ghost a giant former inmate floating through the halls.

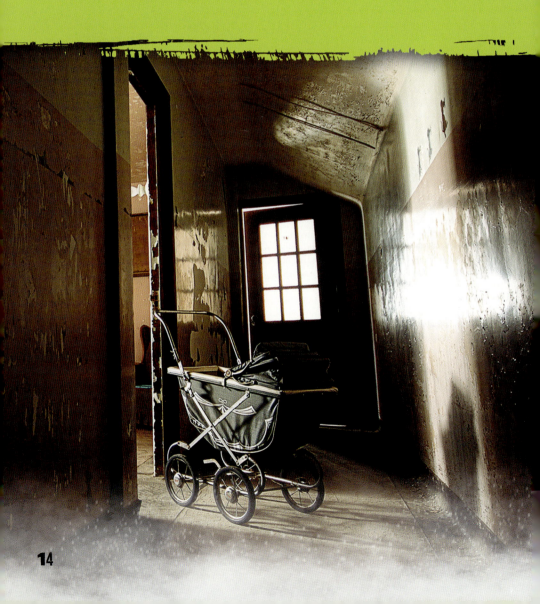

The Trans-Allegheny Asylum in West Virginia was home to over 2,400 patients. But it could only handle 250. Patients were subjected to **inhumane** conditions. It closed in 1994, but the main building still stands today.

Beechworth Asylum in Australia saw more than 9,000 patients die. It closed in 1995. Locals have seen faces in windows and the sound of bone chilling laughter in the abandoned building.

Danvers Asylum was built in 1878 in Massachusetts. After more than 100 years of **overpopulation**, it closed. Yet, reports of flickering lights and unexplained sounds continue to this day.

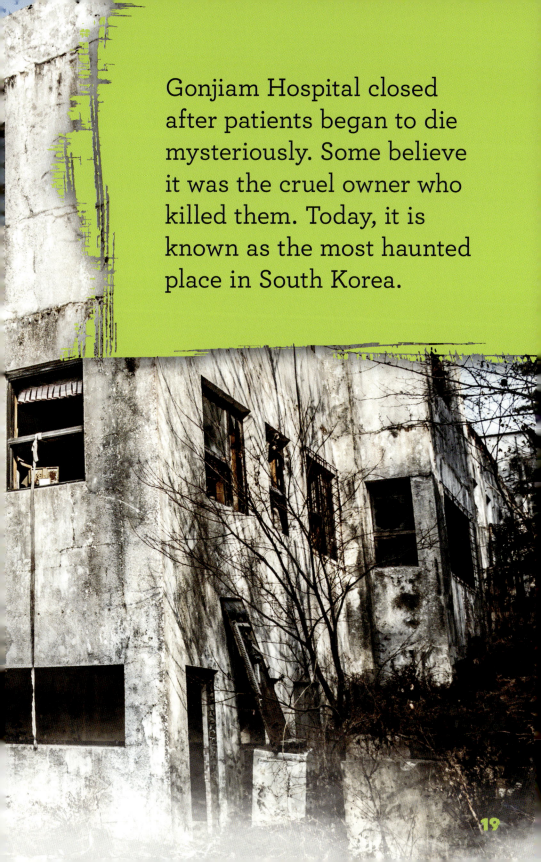

Gonjiam Hospital closed after patients began to die mysteriously. Some believe it was the cruel owner who killed them. Today, it is known as the most haunted place in South Korea.

# THE MEDIA

Haunted asylums are a core setting for horror movies. *Session 9* was filmed in Danvers Asylum. The actors and crew experienced several **supernatural** events while shooting the film.

Many ghost hunting shows investigate abandoned asylums. A majority of the time they are shells of buildings full of shadows and horrifying secrets of the past.

# GLOSSARY

**civilization** – cities or populated areas where modern life takes place.

**disorder** – a disruption of functioning behavior and health.

**inhumane** – lacking pity, kindness, or mercy for people.

**Medieval** – of or belonging to the Middle Ages. The Middle Ages was a period in European history from about 500 CE to 1500 CE.

**overpopulation** – when a place is populated in excess.

**supernatural** – a force beyond scientific logic and the laws of nature.

**ward** – one of the parts into which a hospital is divided for different purposes.

# ONLINE RESOURCES

Booklinks
NONFICTION NETWORK
FREE! ONLINE NONFICTION RESOURCES

To learn more about haunted asylums, please visit **abdobooklinks.com** or scan this QR code. These links are routinely monitored and updated to provide the most current information available.

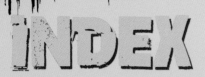

Australia 16

Beechworth Asylum 16

Danvers Asylum 17, 20

Gonjiam Hospital 19

Massachusetts 17

Medieval era 9

Narrenturm 12

New York 14

Persia 9

Rolling Hills Asylum 14

*Session 9* (movie) 20

South Korea 19

Trans-Allegheny Asylum 15

West Virginia 15